SMART ABOUT
The Arts

Hooray
for
Ballet!

by Elizabeth Carr

By Margaret Frith
Illustrated by Amanda Haley

Grosset & Dunlap • New York

For Elizabeth, my favorite ballerina—M.F.
To my parents, for encouraging my love of the arts—A.H.

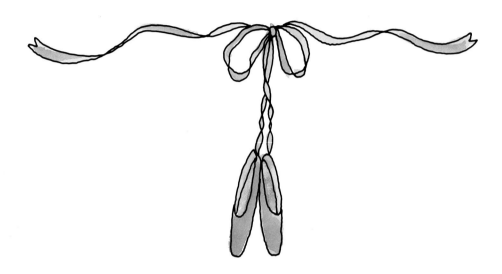

Acknowledgments
We thank Daniel Ulbricht of the New York City Ballet for "modeling"
and Costas for his wonderful photos.

Photo Credits: Front cover: Sleeping Beauty. Martha Swope/Timepix; p 4, 5, 10, 31(right) D. Dorfman; p 7: Bibliotheque Nationale, Paris, France/Giraudon-Bridgeman Art Library; p 12: "The Four Temperaments". Jean-Pierre Bonnefous and members of the New York City Ballet. Choreography: George Balanchine © The Balanchine Trust. Music: Paul Hinoewith./ Photo: Costas; p 15 " Swan Lake". Darci Kistler. Choreography: George Balanchine © The Balanchine Trust. Music: Peter Tchaikovsky. /Photo: Costas; p 17 "Swan Lake". Darci Kistler and Igor Zelensky. Choreography: George Balanchine © The Balanchine Trust. Music: Peter Tchaikovsky./Photo: Costas; page 28 (top left): "Emeralds". Karin von Aroldingen and Sean Lavery. Choreography: George Balanchine © The Balanchine Trust. Music: Gabriel Faure. /Photo: Costas; Page 28 (top right): "Firebird". Lourdes Lopez and Erlands Zieminch. Choreography: George Balanchine and Jerome Robbins © The Balanchine Trust. Music: Igor Stravinsky. /Photo: Costas; 28 (bottom): "Harlequinade". Choreography: George Balanchine © The Balanchine Trust. Music: Ricardo Drigo. /Photo: Costas; Page 29 (top): "Stravinsky Violin Concerto". Wendy Whelan and Jock Soto. Choreography: George Balanchine © The Balanchine Trust. Music: Igor Stravinsky. /Photo: Costas; p 29 (bottom): "Copélia". New York City Ballet and School of American Ballet students. Choreography: George Balanchine © The Balanchine Trust. Music: Léo Delibes. /Photo: Costas; p 30: "The Nutcracker". New York City Ballet and students of the School of American Ballet. Choreography: George Balanchine © The Balanchine Trust. Music: Peter Tchaikovsky. /Photo: Costas; p 31(left): Daniel Ulbricht at School of American Ballet. /Photo: Costas.

Text copyright © 2003 by Margaret Frith. Illustrations copyright © 2003 by Amanda Haley. All rights reserved. Published by Grosset & Dunlap, a division of Penguin Putnam Books for Young Readers, 345 Hudson Street, New York, NY 10014. GROSSET & DUNLAP is a trademark of Penguin Putnam Inc. Published simultaneously in Canada. Manufactured in China

Library of Congress Cataloging-in-Publication Data is available
ISBN 0-448-42884-9 (pbk)   A B C D E F G H I J
ISBN 0-448-43155-6 (GB)   A B C D E F G H I J

From the desk of
Ms. Brandt

Dear Class,
  We have been learning about so many exciting events from the past. Now you may choose a subject that is of special interest to you for your report.
  You may write about something that happened thousands of years ago or about something that happened not so very long ago - maybe when your parents or your grandparents were your age. It's up to you!

  Here are some questions you might want to think about:

🍎 What made you pick your topic?

🍎 Did you learn anything that really surprised you?

  Good luck and have fun!
                            Ms. Brandt

My First Ballet

Lincoln Center

My uncle is a ballet dancer in New York City. So I decided to do my report on ballet. A lot of kids probably think that ballet dancing is just for girls, but it's not.

Uncle Tim took me to see my first ballet. It is called *Swan Lake*. It's about a princess who turns into a swan and falls in love with a prince.

Here we are at Lincoln Center.

The dancers were like acrobats and dancers at the same time. They twirled, jumped, leaped, glided, and flew across the stage, telling the story without saying a word. Wow!

Uncle Tim knows that I love to play soccer. (He has come to my games.) He says that taking ballet lessons will make me stronger and faster when I play.

Me in my soccer uniform.

My ticket for "Swan Lake."

How Ballet Began

Uncle Tim sent me a book about ballet before we went to see *Swan Lake*. I read that ballet dancing started in Italy about five hundred years ago. *Balletto* means "little dance" in Italian.

People began dancing in France, too—right in the palace of the king and queen. Some of the French kings loved to dance. One king, Louis the Fourteenth, once danced in a ballet that lasted all night!

The king had a tennis court inside. It was a good place to put on ballets.

Bravo!

How could the King dance in high heels?

King Louis the 14th

Oops!

tee hee!

Jeté   grand jeté   Plié   tour en l'air   glissade

Plié

Jeté

France was the first place to have a school for ballet. It was in a room in King Louis the Fourteenth's palace. The ballet teacher wrote down the steps and a lot more about how to dance. No one had ever done that before. That's why most ballet steps have French names.

brisé   Cabriole   entrechat   fouetté en tournant

In the early days men danced all the parts. They wore long skirts and wigs to look like ladies.

I feel silly.

Guess where people went the craziest over ballet? Russia. The royal family liked ballet so much that they even started talking to each other in French.

Russia's ballet schools became the most famous in the world, especially The Bolshoi Ballet School in Moscow. It began in 1774. It is not only a school. It has a "company." That's what you call the group of dancers who perform together on stage. The Bolshoi Ballet travels all over the world.

The Bolshoi was the first company to dance "Swan Lake."

The New York City Ballet

Today most ballet schools still teach ballet the same way the Russian schools did. Lots of Uncle Tim's teachers at the School of American Ballet came from Russia, just like George Balanchine, the man who started the school. He was also in charge of the New York City Ballet. Mr. Balanchine was a young dancer in Russia. But he loved making up ballets even more than dancing. His ballets made the New York City Ballet really famous. They were new and exciting.

Mr. Balanchine made up over 400 ballets!

#299

#25

#56

#155

#1

The Choreographer

A ballet usually begins with the choreographer who makes up the dances and writes down the steps for the dancers to follow. A dance on paper looks something like music notes in a songbook.

Spin this way! No! Spin the other way!

Our soccer coach draws the plays for our games on paper, too.

The Music

And that brings me to the music. It is really important in a ballet. Uncle Tim says the more he feels the music, the better he dances.

The choreographer may use music that somebody else has already written. Or the choreographer may ask a composer to write special music just for that ballet. That's what happened with *Swan Lake*.

The famous Russian composer Peter Ilich Tchaikovsky was asked to make up the music. He had never written music for people to dance to. But he turned out to be very good at it. He went on to do the music for two other famous ballets.

Tchaikovsky "The Nutcracker"

Tchaikovsky "The Sleeping Beauty"

Prokofiev "Cinderella"

Stravinsky "The Firebird"

Cinderella

Sleeping Beauty

Firebird

Many ballets, especially ones from the early days, have stories from a folktale or a fairytale, like *Cinderella*. The story of *Swan Lake* came from a German tale.

But a ballet may not have a story. It may just show a mood or feeling. Lots of ballets made up today are like that.

But no matter where the ballet comes from, it is the dancers and the music together who bring it alive on stage.

That's how I felt when I saw *Swan Lake*. It's coming next!

Photo: Costas.

"The Four Temperaments"

Mr. Balanchine made up this ballet about 4 feelings. Sad, Happy, Calm, Angry.

I am sad... I am happy... I am calm... I am MAD!!!

Swan Lake ❀ The Cast

Odette
the Swan Princess

*She is under an evil spell.
She is good.*

Odile

*She is the daughter of the evil
magician. She is bad.*

(*The same ballerina dances both parts.*)

Prince
Siegfried

*The ballet begins
on his birthday at the castle.*

Queen
Mother

*She wants
Siegfried to pick
a wife.*

Evil Magician

*His name is Baron
von Rothbart. He made
the magic spell.*

Swan Maidens

*They are Odette's friends.
They are under the
spell, too.*

Siegfried's Friends

*They go hunting
with the prince.*

Robbie Jack/CORBIS

The ballet starts on Prince Siegfried's birthday. His mom, the Queen, tells him it is time for him to get married. He has to choose a wife at a fancy ball the next night. Siegfried is not so happy about this because he is not in love with anybody. He decides to go hunting with his friends. As they ride off, some swans fly overhead.

The Queen points to her wedding ring. That means "Get Married, Son!" Talking without words is mime.

The Prince and his friends get to a lake deep in the forest just before midnight. Siegfried sees a swan come out of the lake and turn into a beautiful princess. Her name is Odette.

When the ballerina is Odette, she dances slowly and gracefully.

Odette tells Siegfried that she and the other swans are under the spell of an evil magician. They are swans all day and real girls between midnight and dawn. The only way to break the spell is for someone to fall in love with her and marry her.

The Swan girls are the "Corps de Ballet."

Well, Odette and Siegfried fall in love right away. He tells her to come to the ball the next night. That's where he will ask her to marry him. They dance together until dawn. The swan girls dance, too.

Photo: Costas

The star ballerina is the "Prima ballerina." The star man dancer is the "premier danseur."

Julie Lemberger/CORBIS

So far so good. But at the ball things get really messed up. A girl dressed in black shows up. She looks just like Odette. But guess what? She is the daughter of the evil magician. Even her name is almost the same as Odette's. It is Odile.

When the ballerina is Odile, she dances fast, turning and turning and turning!

The trouble is Siegfried thinks Odile *is* Odette. He asks her to marry him. She says yes. He hears wings beating at the window. He looks up and sees Odette. He knows he has made a BIG mistake.

Sad Ending

Siegfried runs to the lake and finds Odette. Together they jump into the lake and drown. It's a really sad ending. But it is brave, too, because this breaks the spell and saves the other girls from being swans forever.

Happy Ending

true Love!

Oh, thank goodness

Robbie Jack/CORBIS

I read that another choreographer made up a happy ending to *Swan Lake*. Siegfried kills the evil magician, and everyone lives happily ever after. But most *Swan Lakes* have the sad ending.

Choreographers have also added new, harder steps to *Swan Lake*. Now Siegfried does exciting jumps and spins without Odette or Odile. When a person dances alone, it is called a solo.

Girls' Costumes

Ballerinas wear skirts called "tutus." My book didn't say exactly why a ballet skirt is called a tutu, but I like this story best. It may come from the French word "cucu," which is baby talk for "rear end." And tutu rhymes with "cucu."

The white tutus in *Swan Lake* are so light they look like feathers. The swan girls wear real feathers in their hair. But I think they look like swans because of the way they move and flutter.

A classical tutu is short.   A romantic tutu is long.

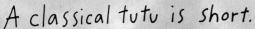

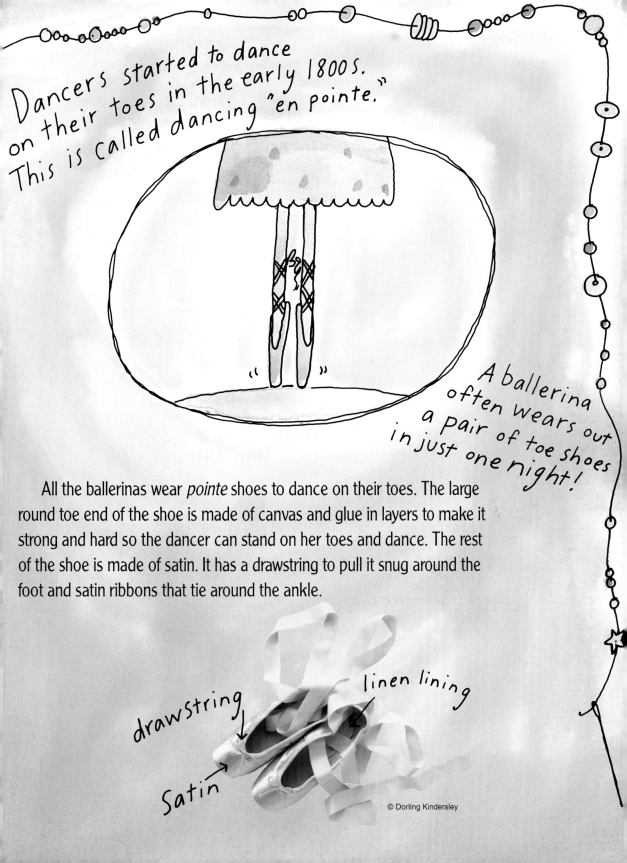

Dancers started to dance on their toes in the early 1800s. This is called dancing "en pointe."

A ballerina often wears out a pair of toe shoes in just one night!

All the ballerinas wear *pointe* shoes to dance on their toes. The large round toe end of the shoe is made of canvas and glue in layers to make it strong and hard so the dancer can stand on her toes and dance. The rest of the shoe is made of satin. It has a drawstring to pull it snug around the foot and satin ribbons that tie around the ankle.

drawstring

linen lining

Satin

... and Guys' Costumes

I know... not very fancy.

The men dancers don't dance on their toes like ballerinas do. They wear ballet slippers. It would be very hard to lift up a ballerina standing on your toes, or to jump high up into the air the way they do.

The men's costumes usually aren't as fancy as the women's. They mostly wear tights on stage. If they are a prince or something, like in *Swan Lake*, their tops might be fancy. And in *Puss in Boots* and *Tales of Beatrix Potter* they get to dress as animals in very elaborate costumes!

This is Peter Rabbit from "Tales of Beatrix Potter."

Robbie Jack/CORBIS

Ballet Class

I was surprised when Uncle Tim told me that he still goes to ballet class almost every day. After all, he knows the dance steps already. But he said that classes keep him in shape, and he needs to practice, just like the way I need to practice soccer.

The very first thing my uncle learned was the five positions for the arms and the feet. They are like the ABCs of ballet.

The Five Positions

First   Second   Third   Fourth   Fifth

Ballet

I got to watch a girls' class. It was in a big room with a wooden floor, mirrors on all the walls, and a wooden bar around three walls. It is called the barre.

This is what dancers wear for classes.

Classes

The teacher stood in front near the piano player. The dancers warmed up at the barre, stretching their arms, backs, legs, and feet. They looked in the mirror to see if they were in the right position.

I saw Uncle Tim's friends do these steps in class.

plié
(plee-ay)

arabesque
(ara-besk)

grand jeté
(gron jeh-tay)

My favorite

I cut these pictures out of ballet magazines. They are some of my favorites. I saw dancers do some of these steps in the class.

The ballerina's green romantic tutu is so beautiful. The ballet is called "Emeralds."

I like the fiery red costumes in "The Firebird."

What a "leap"!

P·h·O·t·O·S

Photo: Costas.

This ballet is called the "Stravinsky Violin Concerto"

Photo: Costas.

These girls don't look much older than me.

At the end of the class I met my uncle's friend Sarah. She has danced in *The Nutcracker*. It has many parts for young dancers. Once I saw *The Nutcracker* on television. I hope I get to see it live on stage sometime.

Guess what! Sarah gave me one of her ballet slippers to take home. She told me that's what the star, or "prima ballerina," does sometimes when someone visits her backstage at the end of the ballet. Sarah hopes she'll be a prima ballerina someday.

Sarah autographed her ballet shoe for me.

Sarah

This is Uncle Tim in his class. I wish I could leap that high!

This is me

Photo: Costas.

Now I'm thinking about taking ballet lessons because it will help me play soccer better. I am the goalie. I need to be fast, to jump high, and to keep my balance.

I don't think I will ever dance in a real ballet like my Uncle Tim. But I will think of him every time I leap up and reach for the ball.

Some Stuff about taking
Ballet Lessons

- Most kids start lessons when they are around eight years old.
- Boys wear black tights with white T-shirts and black ballet slippers.
- Girls wear leotards with pink tights and pink slippers.
- Girls don't dance on their toes until they are older. You have to be really strong or you will hurt yourself.
- Most classes last for an hour to two hours.
- Lots of kids take music lessons, too—piano, guitar, singing.
- You don't get into a company until you are about eighteen.
- The great dancers still take classes every day! So I guess lessons are really important!

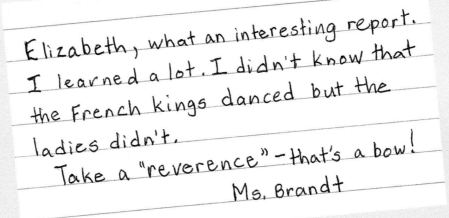

Elizabeth, what an interesting report. I learned a lot. I didn't know that the French kings danced but the ladies didn't.
Take a "reverence" – that's a bow!
Ms. Brandt